What is a dog's favorite Easter treat?
Jelly bones!

Why did the Pilgrims eat turkey at Thanksgiving?
They couldn't get the moose in the oven!

Why does Santa use reindeer to pull his sleigh?
Because the elephants kept crashing through the roof!

By Jim Davis
Published by Ballantine Books:

GARFIELD AT LARGE
GARFIELD GAINS WEIGHT
GARFIELD BIGGER THAN LIFE
GARFIELD WEIGHS IN
GARFIELD TAKES THE CAKE
GARFIELD EATS HIS HEART OUT
GARFIELD SITS AROUND THE HOUSE
GARFIELD TIPS THE SCALES
GARFIELD LOSES HIS FEET
GARFIELD MAKES IT BIG
GARFIELD ROLLS ON
GARFIELD OUT TO LUNCH
GARFIELD FOOD FOR THOUGHT
GARFIELD SWALLOWS HIS PRIDE
GARFIELD WORLDWIDE
GARFIELD ROUNDS OUT
GARFIELD CHEWS THE FAT
GARFIELD GOES TO WAIST
GARFIELD HANGS OUT
GARFIELD TAKES UP SPACE
GARFIELD BY THE POUND
GARFIELD SAYS A MOUTHFUL
GARFIELD KEEPS HIS CHINS UP
GARFIELD TAKES HIS LICKS
GARFIELD HITS THE BIG TIME

GARFIELD'S BIG FAT HAIRY JOKE BOOK
GARFIELD'S SON OF BIG FAT HAIRY JOKES
GARFIELD'S BIG FAT SCARY JOKE BOOK
GARFIELD'S INSULTS, PUT-DOWNS & SLAMS
GARFIELD'S BIG FAT HOLIDAY JOKE BOOK

GARFIELD'S BIG FAT HOLIDAY JOKE BOOK

Created by
Jim Davis

Written by
Jim Kraft and Mark Acey

BALLANTINE BOOKS • NEW YORK

Copyright © 1994 by PAWS, INCORPORATED

All rights reserved under International and Pan-American Copyright Conventions. Published in the United States of America by Ballantine Books, a division of Random House, Inc., New York, and simultaneously in Canada by Random House of Canada Limited, Toronto.

Library of Congress Catalog Card Number: 94-94415

Printed in Canada

ISBN 0-345-38955-7

First Edition: December 1994

10 9 8 7 6 5 4 3 2

CONTENTS

Snappy Holidays!

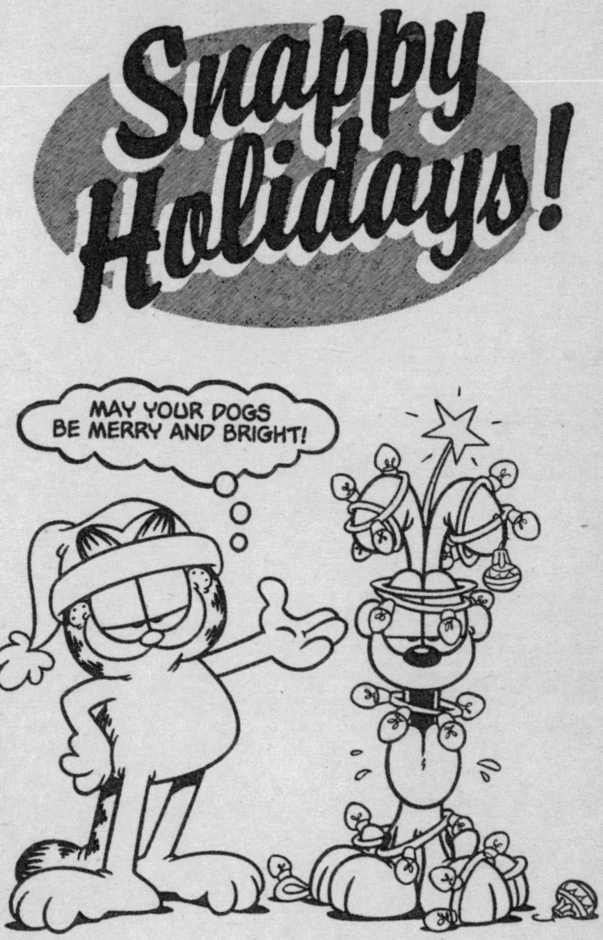
MAY YOUR DOGS
BE MERRY AND BRIGHT!

If you dropped Garfield into a bowl of eggnog, what would you get?
Out of there as fast as you can!

Why is Garfield at the beach like Christmas?
They both have sandy claws!

What has four legs, a red nose, and flies?
Rudolph the Red-Nosed Roadkill!

Why does Santa hire elves to make his toys?
Because they make short work of the job!

3

What's the difference between a snowman and Odie?
One has snow brains and the other has no brains!

What is Frosty's favorite dinner?
Spaghetti and snowballs.

Knock, knock!
Who's there?
Earl.
Earl who?
Earl I want for Christmas is lots of everything!

Why does Santa use reindeer to pull his sleigh?
Because the elephants kept crashing through the roof!

Why did Odie fetch Jon's hedge clippers on Christmas
    Eve?
Because he heard Jon say it was time to trim the tree.

What would you get if you crossed a pig with a Christmas tree?
A porker pine!

What is Tarzan's favorite Christmas carol?
"Jungle Bells."

Why did the elf paint himself green?
He was moonlighting as a leprechaun.

Why do we kiss under the mistletoe?
Because it's more fun than shaking hands!

Did you hear about the author elf?
He only wrote short stories!

What would you get if you crossed Jon with the Little Drummer Boy?
The Little Dumber Boy!

What is Garfield's favorite Christmas film?
It's A Wonderful Lunch!

Santa: "Those toymakers I hired are just not working out."
Mrs. Claus: "Like they say, good elf is hard to find."

What is a vampire's favorite Christmas song?
"I'm Dreaming of a Bite Christmas."

What amphibian do we hang in doorways at Christmas?
Mistletoad.

What has a red suit, a white beard, and rows of razor-sharp teeth?
Santa Jaws.

Knock, knock!
Who's there?
Doc.
Doc who?
Doc the halls with boughs of holly!

Why is Santa like a busy gardener?
Because all he does is hoe, hoe, hoe!

What would you get if you crossed Santa Claus with
    Garfield?
A jolly old elf who fills your stocking and empties your
    fridge!

What kind of dog spends all New Year's Day watching
    football?
A bowl dog!

What is Santa's favorite Easter candy?
Jolly beans!

What does a naughty genie get for Christmas?
A lamp of coal!

What would you call it if your wedding day was
    December 25?
A Marry Christmas!

In the Middle Ages, what did most people get for
    Christmas?
The plague!

Who had a beard, webbed feet, and wrote *A Christmas
    Carol*?
Charles Duckens!

What's red and white and blue all over?
A candy cane holding its breath!

What do you call a fear of being trapped in a chimney
    with a fat man?
Santa Claustrophobia!

Jon: "Do you like the present I gave you, Garfield?"
Garfield: "Yes, I'd like to return it."

Where does Santa Claus keep his red suit?
In his Santa Clauset.

What's red and white and green all over?
An airsick Santa Claus!

Jon: "We must remember to leave something for Santa
    tonight."
Garfield: "Yeah. Bribe money."

Why does Santa have a house at the North Pole?
Because he's too fat to squeeze into an igloo!

What's red and white and full of holes?
Swiss Kringle!

Santa: "What do you want for Christmas, young man?"
Boy: "Well, there's a certain thing I'd really like."
Santa: "What thing is that?"
Boy: "*Every*thing!"

What would you get if you crossed Santa with a
      giraffe?
St. Neck!

What would you get if you crossed one of Santa's help-
      ers with the King of Rock 'n' Roll?
Elfis Presley!

What happened when Garfield swallowed the Christ-
      mas decorations?
He needed a tinselectomy!

What has fins, a tail, and is mailed to you at Christmas?
A Christmas cod!

Jon: "Garfield, they asked me to sing solo in the Christmas choir!"
Garfield: "Yeah, solo that no one can hear you!"

What's the difference between Garfield and a Christmas stocking?
One is large, soft, and stuffed with holiday goodies, and the other's a sock!

What did Santa say to his misbehaving reindeer?
"Shape up or I'll get a gnu crew."

Why don't elves play in the NBA?
They just don't measure up!

Knock, knock!
Who's there?
Anna.
Anna who?
Anna partridge in a pear tree!

What would you get if you crossed St. Nick with Jon
    Arbuckle?
Santa Clod!

What does Garfield wish everyone for the holidays?
Pizza on earth!

What is Santa's favorite American state?
Idaho-ho-ho!

What do Santa's helpers make the day before Christmas?
Eight dollars an hour plus time and a half for overtime!

Why did Garfield hit Odie with a bell on January 1?
He wanted to ring in the New Year!

What are New Year's resolutions?
Things that go in one year and out the other!

Why does snow fall in the winter?
Because it would melt in the summer!

What is a monster's favorite Christmas poem?
"The Fright Before Christmas"!

What is a ghost's favorite Christmas carol?
"We Wish You a Scary Christmas!"

What would you have if Santa brought you a kitten and
    a puppy?
A meowy Christmas and a yappy New Year!

13

Why was Santa's sick helper reluctant to go to the hospital?
Because he didn't have elf insurance!

What has four legs, a hump, and is found at the North Pole?
A lost camel!

What goes "Ho-Ho-Ho-Swish"?
Santa drilling a jump shot!

Girl 1: "Do you like *The Nutcracker Suite*?"
Girl 2: "I'm sugarplum crazy about it!"

Is there a city at the North Pole?
No, just an ice burg!

What happens when Christmas angels meet?
They both say, "Halo!"

Where does Christmas come before Thanksgiving?
In the dictionary!

Basically Blarney

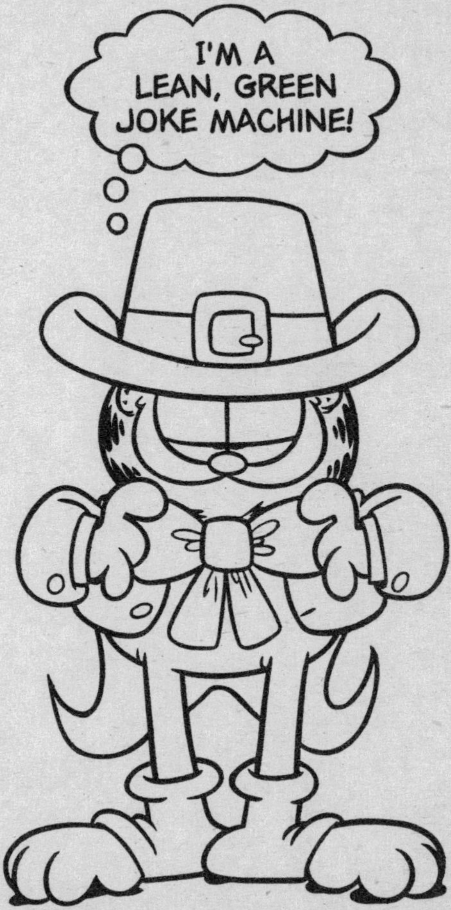
I'M A LEAN, GREEN JOKE MACHINE!

What kind of music does a leprechaun band play?
Shamrock 'n' roll!

Teacher: "Why did St. Patrick drive the snakes out of
    Ireland?"
Student: "Because it was too far for them to crawl."

What would you get if you crossed a leprechaun with
    a frog?
A little green man with a croak of gold!

What did the leprechaun say to the elf?
"How's the weather up there?"

What would you get if you crossed an Irishman with a
    basketball star?
Eire Jordan!

What do you call a rainy day in Ireland?
A bad Eire day!

Irishman: "How long will you be staying in Ireland?"
Tourist: "Just one day, I'm afraid."
Irishman: "Like they say: 'Eire today, gone tomor-
    row!' "

Did you hear about the leprechaun who went to jail?
He was a leprecon!

Jon: "I need to find something green for St. Patrick's
    Day."
Garfield: "Check the meat loaf in the back of the
    fridge!"

How did the leprechaun get to the moon?
In a shamrocket!

What would you get if you crossed a purple dinosaur
    with an Irish landmark?
The Barney Stone!

Knock, knock!
Who's there?
Irish.
Irish who?
Irish you a happy St. Patrick's Day!

What do you get when two leprechauns have a conver-
    sation?
A lot of small talk!

Why can't Odie march in the St. Patrick's Day parade?
Because he can't march and breathe at the same time.

What's the best way to get a letter to Ireland?
Send it Eire mail!

What would you get if you crossed Odie with a famous
     Irish actor?
Peter O'Drool!

Knock, knock!
Who's there?
Warren.
Warren who?
Warren anything green today?

What's big and purple and lies next to Ireland?
Grape Britain!

Knock, knock!
Who's there?
Aaron.
Aaron who?
Aaron go bragh and all that Irish talk!

What would you get if you crossed Odie with Ireland's capital city?
Duh-blin!

What would you get if you crossed a dog with an Irish instrument?
A bagpup!

Did you hear the one about the Irish peat?
You can dig it!

What did the leprechaun put in the candy machine?
A lepre-coin!

What baseball position do leprechauns usually play?
*Short*stop!

Knock, knock!
Who's there?
O'Flynn.
O'Flynn who?
O'Flynn the door and let me in!

Why is Ireland like a wine bottle?
Because it has a Cork in it!

What do you call a leprechaun who disappears?
A lepre-gone!

What would you get if you crossed a leprechaun with
a yellow vegetable?
Lepre-corn!

What do you call a clumsy Irish dance?
A jig mistake!

What would you get if you crossed an Irish landmark
with a Stone Age cartoon character?
Blarney Rubble!

What would you get if you crossed a leprechaun with
   a Texan?
A pot of chili at the end of the rainbow!

What's smaller than a leprechaun's whisker?
A dog's brain!

What would you get if you crossed an Irish holiday
   with Garfield?
St. *Fat*rick's Day!

What would you get if you crossed Christmas with St.
   Patrick's Day?
St. O'Claus!

Are people jealous of the Irish?
Sure, they're green with envy!

What would you get if you crossed Quasimodo with an
     Irish football player?
The Halfback of Notre Dame!

"I married an Irishman on St. Patrick's Day."
"Oh, really?"
"No, O'Reilly!"

Why did the leprechaun stand on the potato?
To keep from falling in the stew!

Do leprechauns make good secretaries?
Sure, they're great at shorthand!

How did the leprechaun beat the Irishman to the pot
     of gold?
He took a shortcut!

What do leprechauns love to barbecue?
Short ribs!

Why are leprechauns so hard to get along with?
Because they're very short-tempered!

What does Ireland have more of than any other country?
Irishmen!

What did one Irish ghost say to the other?
"Top o' the moaning!"

Where would you find a leprechaun baseball team?
In the Little League!

What do you call a leprechaun's vacation home?
A lepre-condo!

What do you call a leprechaun with a sore throat?
A streprechaun!

What did St. Patrick say to the snakes?
He told them to "hiss off!"

Are there many selfish people in Ireland?
Yes, because in Ireland, "I" always comes first!

Did you hear about the man who wanted to sound
    Irish?
He decided to go for brogue!

What would you get if you crossed a leprechaun with
    a seashell?
A lepre-conch!

What do you call a performance by a leprechaun band?
A lepre-concert!

26

Knock, knock!
Who's there?
Don.
Don who?
Don be puttin' down the Irish now!

Knock, knock!
Who's there?
Pat.
Pat who?
Pat your coat on, and let's go to the St. Patrick's Day
    parade!

Why did the Irish tenor stand on the chair?
So he could reach the high notes!

What would you get if you crossed Odie with a well-
    known Irish ballad?
"O Dummy Boy"!

What would you get if you crossed a leprechaun with
    a bathroom?
A lepre-john!

What's little and green and goes two hundred miles
   per hour?
A leprechaun in a blender!

Cook 1: "What do you think of my Irish stew?"
Cook 2: "It could use a pinch of Gaelic."

What's little and green and stuck to your bumper?
A leprechaun who didn't look both ways.

Did you hear about the leprechaun who worked at the
   diner?
He was a *short*-order cook!

What's six feet tall, green, and has a crock of gold?
A leprechaun with a gland problem!

Do leprechauns get angry when you make fun of their
   height?
Yeah, but only a little!

LIFE, LIBERTY, AND THE PURSUIT OF SILLINESS

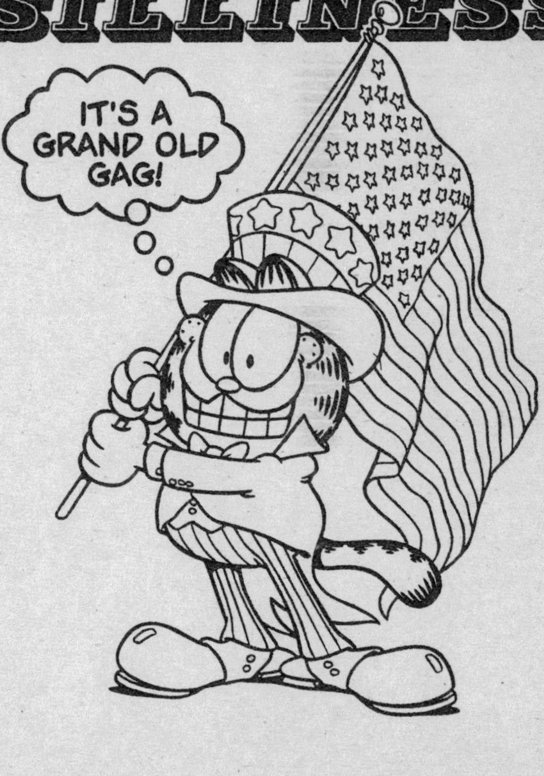
IT'S A GRAND OLD GAG!

Teacher: "Where was the Declaration of Independence signed?"
Student: "On the bottom!"

Teacher: "Why does our country have a two-party system?"
Student: "So we can have one party on Friday and one on Saturday!"

Teacher: "Why did Paul Revere take a midnight ride?"
Student: "Because he missed the 10:30 bus."

What would you get if you crossed one of the Founding Fathers with a famous monster?
Benjamin Franklinstein!

What would you get if you crossed a vegetable with the first president of the United States?
George Squashington!

Why did Paul Revere yell "The Martians are coming!"?
His horse had just kicked him in the head!

What did George Washington say to his army at Valley Forge?
"Sorry, men. The flights to Florida are all booked up!"

What would you get if you crossed the American national bird with Snoopy?
A bald beagle!

What would you get if you crossed a colonial hairpiece with a teepee?
A powdered wigwam!

What's red, white, blue, and green?
A patriotic pickle!

What would you get if you crossed the first signer of
    the Declaration of Independence with a rooster?
John Hancock-a-doodle-doo!

What quacks, has webbed feet, and betrays his coun-
    try?
Beneduck Arnold!

What would you get if you crossed John Paul Jones
    with Garfield?
A navy captain who says, "I have not yet begun to eat!"

What did Paul Revere say at the end of his ride?
"I gotta get a softer saddle!"

What protest by a group of dogs occurred in 1773?
The Boston Flea Party!

What happened as a result of the Stamp Act?
The Americans licked the British!

Why did Paul Revere ride his horse from Boston to
    Lexington?
Because the horse was too heavy to carry!

Why did the British cross the Atlantic?
To get to the other tide!

What do you call a parade of German mercenaries?
A Hessian procession!

What would you get if you crossed a patriot with a
    small curly-haired dog?
Yankee Poodle!

Did you hear the one about the Liberty Bell?
Yeah, it cracked me up!

What did the visitor say as he left the Statue of Liberty?
"Keep in torch!"

What's big, cracked, and carries your luggage?
The Liberty Bellhop!

What ghost haunted King George III?
The spirit of '76!

What would you get if you crossed Patrick Henry with Garfield?
A patriot who says, "Give me lasagna or give me death!"

What would you get if you crossed George Washington with cattle feed?
The Fodder of Our Country!

What's red, white, blue, and almost as ugly as a dog?
A revolutionary warthog!

What did one flag say to the other flag?
Nothing. It just waved!

What's red, white, blue, and gross?
Uncle Spam!

What's red, white, black and blue?
Uncle Sam falling down the steps!

Where did George Washington buy his hatchet?
At the chopping mall!

What kind of tea did the American colonists thirst for?
Liberty!

What was General Washington's favorite tree?
The infantry!

Which colonists told the most jokes?
*Pun*sylvanians!

What would you get if you crossed Washington's home
with nasty insects?
Mt. Vermin!

What has feathers, webbed feet, and certain inalien-
able rights?
The Ducklaration of Independence!

Why did the duck say "Bang!"?
Because he was a firequacker!

Teacher: "The Declaration of Independence was written in Philadelphia. True or false?"
Student: "False! It was written in ink!"

Did you know that one of Odie's ancestors served in the Continental Army?
He was a drool sergeant!

Who is Garfield's favorite Founding Father?
Yawn Adams.

Why did Washington win the battle of Trenton?
Because the enemy soldiers were Hessian around!

What would you get if you crossed Odie with one of Washington's officers?
Baron von Steupid!

What did a patriot put on his dry skin?
Revo-lotion!

What would you get if you crossed Odie with the Father of Our Country?
George Washingtongue!

Who is Odie's favorite Founding Father?
Bone Franklin!

What would you get if you crossed Jon with the English king in 1776?
King George the Nerd!

What dance was very popular in 1776?
Indepen-dance!

Which one of Washington's officers had the best sense of humor?
Laughayette!

What is Garfield's favorite picnic event?
The snack race!

Nermal: "How was the food at Jon's Fourth of July picnic?"
Garfield: "The hot dogs were bad and the brats were wurst!"

What did Washington say as he crossed the Delaware?
"Next time I'm going to reserve a seat!"

Teacher: "Why did Washington chop down the cherry tree with his hatchet?"
Student: "Because his mom wouldn't let him play with the chain saw!"

What has four legs, a shiny nose, and fought for England?
Rudolph the Redcoat Reindeer!

What march would you play at a jungle parade?
"Tarzan Stripes Forever"!

What would you get if you crossed Garfield with a red-
    coat?
A bigger target.

Why did the British soldiers wear red coats?
So they could hide in the tomatoes.

Why is the Liberty Bell like a dropped Easter egg?
Because they're both cracked!

Teacher: "Who wrote 'Oh say, can you see?' "
Student: "An eye doctor?"

How is a healthy person like the United States?
They both have good constitutions!

What cat said, "The British are coming! The British are coming!"?
Paw Revere.

What was the craziest battle of the Revolutionary War?
The Battle of Bonkers Hill.

What was Thomas Jefferson's favorite dessert?
Monti-jello!

Teacher: "Which son of old Virginia wrote the Declaration of Independence?"
Student: "I think it was Thomas Jeffer's son."

What did King George think of the American colonists?
He thought they were revolting!

Why were the early American settlers like ants?
Because they lived in colonies.

What famous pig signed the Declaration of Independence?
John Hamcock!

What's the difference between John Adams and Jon Arbuckle?
One was a famous patriot and the other is a famous idiot!

What would you get if you crossed Garfield with a minuteman?
A patriot who's ready to eat at a minute's notice!

What did Betsy Ross eat for breakfast?
Red, white, and blueberry muffins!

Did you hear about the cartoonist in the Continental
    Army?
He was a Yankee doodler!

What would you get if you crossed Odie with Yankee
    Doodle?
Yankee Doofus!

What's red, white, blue and green?
A seasick Uncle Sam!

TURKEY TALK

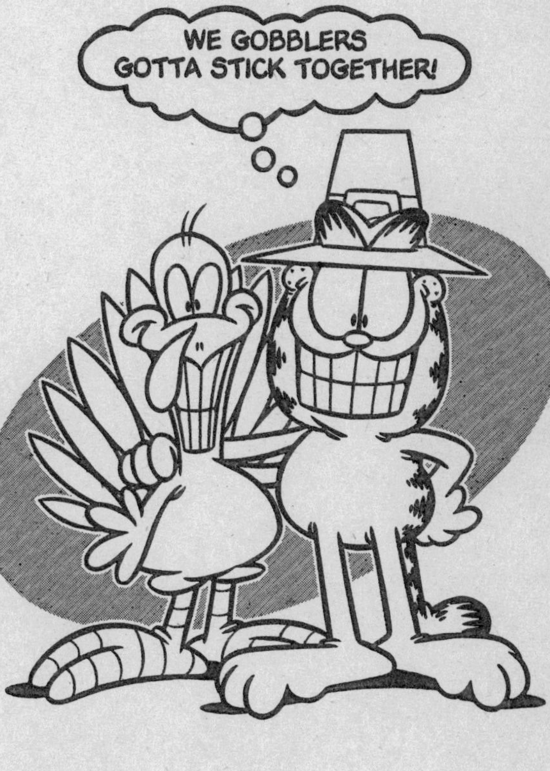
WE GOBBLERS
GOTTA STICK TOGETHER!

Why did the Pilgrims eat turkey on Thanksgiving?
They couldn't get the moose in the oven!

If April showers bring May flowers, what do May flowers bring?
Pilgrims!

What's the best way to stuff a turkey?
Take him out for pizza and ice cream!

What did the turkey say to the turkey hunter?
"Quack! Quack! Quack!"

What does Garfield get after he's eaten way too much
     turkey and dressing?
Dessert, of course!

Why did the Pilgrims create Thanksgiving?
They wanted another excuse to watch football.

Jon: "What should I serve with my famous cranberry
     salad?"
Garfield: "The antidote."

What crime did Garfield commit at Thanksgiving din-
     ner?
Pie-jacking!

Why is Garfield like a Thanksgiving turkey?
Because he's always stuffed!

Why did Garfield think of Thanksgiving when he saw Jon take off his clothes?
Because he saw the turkey undressing!

Teacher: "Where is Plymouth Rock?"
Student: "Right next to Plymouth Bush!"

What would you get if you crossed Odie with a turkey leg?
A dumbstick!

Teacher: "Where did the Pilgrims come from?"
Student: "Their parents, of course!"

Did you hear about the gobbler who bounced around the barnyard?
He was a perky turkey!

Jon: "I was going to serve sweet potatoes with Thanksgiving dinner, but Garfield sat on them.
Liz: "So what are you serving now?"
Jon: "Squash."

What's the difference between Odie and a Thanksgiving parade balloon?
Odie has more air in his head!

What did General Patton do on Thanksgiving?
He gave tanks.

Jon: "You know, Garfield, an ancestor of mine came over on the Mayflower."
Garfield: "Really? Which rat was he?"

What's black and white and red all over?
A Pilgrim with a rash!

How did Albert Einstein celebrate Thanksgiving?
He was very thinkful.

What kind of music did Pilgrim bands play?
Plymouth Rock 'n' roll!

What would you get if you crossed a pickle with an early New England settler?
A Dillgrim!

Teacher: "What did the Indians bring to the first Thanksgiving?"
Student: "Baseballs."
Teacher: "Baseballs?"
Student: "Yeah, they were *Cleveland* Indians!"

Why did Odie turn out the lights during Thanksgiving dinner?
Because Jon said he wanted dark meat!

Why didn't Garfield get a second helping of turkey?
Because he ate it all the first time!

What's the difference between Doc Boy and a turkey?
One is a brainless barnyard lardball and the other is a
     bird.

Why did the Pilgrim shoot the turkey?
Because he was in a fowl mood!

What would you get if you crossed Doc Boy with a
     Thanksgiving dessert?
Bumpkin pie!

What did Garfield say to the Thanksgiving turkey?
"Pleased to eat you!"

What would you get if you crossed a turkey with a
     baked fruit dessert?
Peach gobbler!

How can you tell a male turkey from a female turkey?
The male is the one holding the remote control.

What do you call the dirt on a Pilgrim's hands?
Pilgrime!

What is Garfield's favorite thing to make for Thanksgiving dinner?
Reservations!

How is an undercooked turkey like one of Jon's ideas?
Both of them are half-baked!

Teacher: "Who built the first American car?"
Student: "The Pilgrims."
Teacher: "The Pilgrims?"
Student: "Yeah, they made the Mayflower Compact."

Why was Odie chasing the band in the Thanksgiving parade?
He wanted to bury the trombones!

Teacher: "Why do we have a Thanksgiving holiday?"
Student: "So we know when to start Christmas shopping!"

How many cooks does it take to stuff a turkey?
One, but you really have to squeeze him in!

What November holiday do crabby people celebrate?
Cranksgiving!

What does a Pilgrim call his best friend?
A palgrim.

Teacher: "Why did the Pilgrims sail to America?"
Student: "Maybe they missed their plane."

What would you get if you crossed a turkey with an
    evil spirit?
A poultrygeist!

What's brown and white and flies all over?
Thanksgiving turkey, when you carve it with a chain
    saw!

What happens when Garfield eats too much at Thanks-
    giving?
He gets thick to his stomach!

Why did Garfield get a ticket at Thanksgiving dinner?
He was exceeding the feed limit!

What would you get if you crossed a famous Giant
    with Indian corn?
Willie Maize!

What happened when the turkey met the ax?
He lost his head!

Why was Garfield tickled when he ate the turkey?
Because Jon forgot to pluck the feathers!

Why should you never talk like a turkey?
Because it's bad to use fowl language!

Knock, knock!
Who's there?
Arthur.
Arthur who?
Arthur any leftovers?

What did the Indian call the Pilgrim with a bucket over
   his head?
"Pailface."

What would you get if you crossed a Pilgrim with a
    type of cracker?
A Pilgraham!

How does Garfield like his turkey and stuffing?
In large quantities!

What would you get if you crossed Thanksgiving and
    Easter?
Feaster Sunday!

What is Garfield's favorite place to see a turkey?
On his plate!

What was the main thing the Pilgrims did during the
    first winter?
Starve.

What sign was posted during the first Thanksgiving?
"No Moccasins, No Loincloth, No Service."

What's the key to a great Thanksgiving?
A tur-key, of course!

PARTY HEARTY!

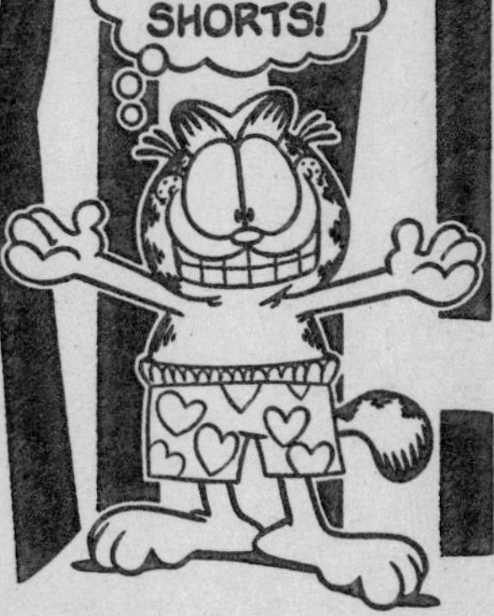

What do farmers give their wives on Valentine's Day?
Hogs and kisses!

What would you get if you crossed Odie with the god
   of love?
A stupid Cupid!

Why did the pig give his girlfriend a box of candy?
It was Valenswine's Day!

Do skunks celebrate Valentine's Day?
Sure, they're very scent-imental!

What did the chocolate syrup say to the ice cream?
"I'm sweet on you!"

What did the French chef give his wife for Valentine's Day?
A hug and a quiche!

What did the paper clip say to the magnet?
"I find you very attractive."

What did the pencil say to the paper?
"I dot my i's on you!"

What would you call a woman who goes out with Jon?
Desperate!

What did one pickle say to the other?
"You mean a great dill to me."

Knock, knock!
Who's there?
Olive.
Olive who?
Olive you!

What did the elephant say to his girlfriend?
"I love you a ton!"

What did the bat say to his girlfriend?
"You're fun to hang around with."

Did you hear about the nearsighted porcupine?
He fell in love with a pincushion!

Liz: "I can't be your valentine for medical reasons."
Jon: "Really?"
Liz: "Yeah, you make me sick!"

What did the boy pig say to the girl pig?
"I'm hog wild about you!"

What did one calculator say to the other?
"How do I love thee? Let me count the ways!"

What did one bell say to the other?
"Be my valenchime!"

What happened when Garfield kissed his one true love?
He left lip prints on the mirror!

What did one monster say to the other?
"Be my valenslime!"

Why did the cannibal break up with his girlfriend?
She didn't suit his taste!

What would you get if you crossed Odie with a valentine card?
A card that says, "I love you drool-ly!"

What did the painter say to her boyfriend?
"I love you with all my art!"

What does a man who loves his car do on February 14?
He gives it a valenshine!

Arlene: "Garfield, do you love me more than you love sleep?"
Garfield: "I can't answer now. It's time for my nap!"

What did the man with the broken leg say to his nurse?
"I've got a crutch on you!"

Did you hear about the romance in the tropical fish tank?
It was a case of guppy love.

What do you call two birds in love?
Tweethearts!

What do you call a very small valentine?
A valentiny!

What did Frankenstein say to his girlfriend?
"Be my valenstein!"

Why did Odie put clothes on the valentines he was sending?
Because Jon said they needed to be ad-dressed!

Why do valentines have hearts on them?
Because spleens would look pretty gross!

What is the most romantic city in England?
Loverpool!

What's red and white and swims in the ocean?
A valentine cod!

Did you hear the one about the phony Cupid?
He was totally bow-gus!

Why is Valentine's Day the best day for a celebration?
Because you can really party hearty!

Why didn't Cupid shoot his arrow at the lawyer's
    heart?
Because even Cupid can't hit a target that small!

What did one oar say to the other?
"Can I interest you in a little row-mance?"

What happened when the man fell in love with his garden?
It made him wed his plants!

What happened when the two angels got married?
They lived harpily ever after!

Why should you send your sweetie a valentine?
Because you always heart the one you love!

Knock, knock!
Who's there?
Howard.
Howard who?
Howard you like a great big kiss?

What does a carpet salesman give his wife for Valentine's Day?
Rugs and kisses!

What would you get if you crossed Cupid with a base-
    ball player?
A glover boy!

What happened when the two tennis players met?
It was lob at first sight!

Why was Liz afraid to accept Jon's valentine present?
Because you should always beware of geeks bearing
    gifts!

What would you get if you crossed Cupid with a meat-
    and-vegetable dish?
Stewpid!

What would you get if you crossed Garfield's true love
    with Jon's true love?
Lizagna!

What did the caveman give his wife on Valentine's Day?
Ughs and kisses!

What did one piece of string say to the other?
"Be my valentwine!"

Why did the kangaroo love the little Australian bear?
Because the bear had many fine koala-ties!

What did one mannequin say to the other?
"I'm warm for your form!"

What did one fir tree say to the other?
"Be my valenpine!"

Knock, knock!
Who's there?
Kisses.
Kisses who?
Kisses your valentine speaking!

What's the difference between Odie and one of Jon's
    dates?
The date is the one with the flea collar.

Then there was the guy who promised his girlfriend a
    diamond for Valentine's Day. So he took her to a
    baseball park!

What do you get when dragons kiss?
Third degree burns of the lips!

What did one light bulb say to the other?
"I love you a whole watt!"

Arlene: "I often think about you, Garfield. How about you?"
Garfield: "Yes, I often think about me, too."

Knock, knock!
Who's there?
Alec.
Alec who?
Alec to kiss your face!

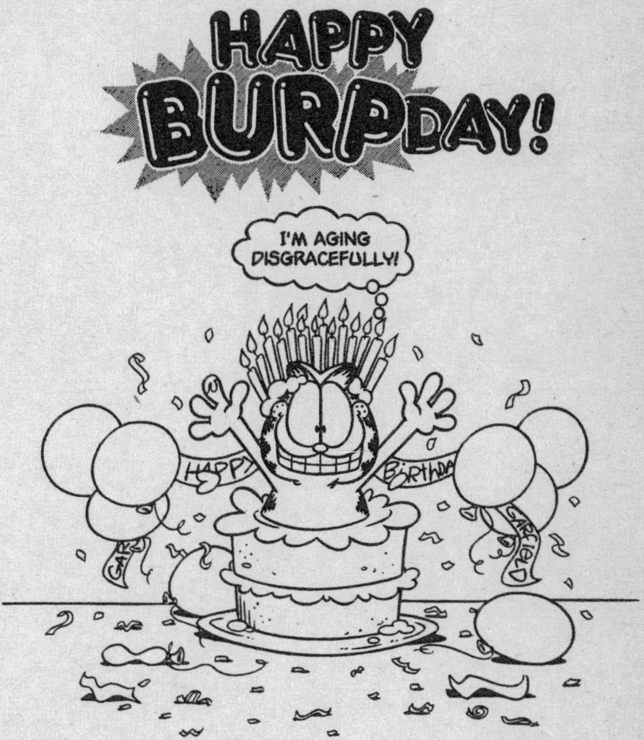
HAPPY BURPDAY!
I'M AGING DISGRACEFULLY!
HAPPY
BIRTHDAY
GARFIELD
GAR

Why does Garfield take extra naps on June 19?
Because he likes to have a nappy birthday!

What is Garfield's favorite party game?
"Pin the Nermal on the Donkey."

Knock, knock!
Who's there?
Mark.
Mark who?
Mark your calendars ... my birthday's just around the
    corner!

What does Garfield always get on his birthday?
Another year older!

Why do we put candles on top of a birthday cake?
Because it's too hard to put them on the bottom!

Why did Odie give Garfield a pair of bunny ears?
He wanted Garfield to have a hoppy birthday!

Knock, knock!
Who's there?
Wanda.
Wanda who?
Wanda wish you a happy birthday!

Why did Odie put the cake in the freezer?
Because Jon told him to ice it.

Why does Garfield act wild and crazy on his birthday?
He's trying to age disgracefully!

Why was Odie standing on his head at the birthday party?
He heard they were having upside-down cake!

What usually comes after Jon lights Garfield's candles?
The fire department.

When is a birthday cake like a golf ball?
When it's been sliced.

What does Garfield get after he's eaten too much ice cream?
More ice cream!

What's the difference between Odie and a birthday candle?
The candle is a thousand times brighter!

77

How can you tell when Garfield's birthday party is
    over?
The riot police go home.

Arlene: "Were any famous men born on your birth-
    day?"
Garfield: "No, only little babies."

For his birthday Jon asked for a heavy sweater. So
    Garfield gave him a sumo wrestler!

What is Garfield's favorite type of present?
Another present!

How does Moby Dick celebrate his birthday?
He has a whale of a party!

Nermal: "When's your birthday?"
Garfield: "June 19."
Nermal: "What year?"
Garfield: "*Every* year!"

What did the birthday balloon say to the pin?
"Hi, Buster."

Knock, knock.
Who's there?
Ben.
Ben who?
Ben over and get your birthday spanking!

Why did Odie hit his birthday cake with a hammer?
Because Jon said it was pound cake!

What did one candle say to the other?
"Don't birthdays burn you up?"

Why couldn't prehistoric man send birthday cards?
The stamps kept falling off the rocks!

Why did Davy Crockett always wear a coonskin cap?
It was a birthday present from his wife!

Where do you find a birthday present for a cat?
In a cat-alogue!

What did the big candle say to the little candle?
"You're too young to go out."

Why did Jon feel warm on his birthday?
Because people kept toasting him!

Why was the birthday cake as hard as a rock?
Because it was marble cake!

Garfield: "What did you get Jon for his birthday?"
Odie: "Pant ... pant!"
Garfield: "Great ... he needs a pair of pants!"

What does a clam do on his birthday?
He shellabrates!

How can you tell that you're getting old?
You go to an antique auction and three people bid on
    you!

What do they serve at birthday parties in heaven?
Angel food cake, of course!

What is an elf's favorite kind of birthday cake?
Shortcake!

What has wings, a long tail, and wears a bow?
A birthday pheasant!

Garfield: "This birthday cake certainly is crunchy."
Arlene: "Maybe you should spit out the plate!"

Is Garfield getting older and wiser?
No, he's getting older and *wider*!

Man 1: "I got my wife a VCP for her birthday."
Man 2: "Don't you mean a VCR?"
Man 1: "No, a VCP ... Very Cheap Present!"

Where does a snowman put his birthday candles?
On his birthday flake!

What does a cat like to eat on his birthday?
Mice cream and cake!

Knock, knock!
Who's there?
Jimmy.
Jimmy who?
Jimmy some ice cream and cake! I'm starving!

Garfield: "I guess I didn't get my birthday wish."
Nermal: "How do you know?"
Garfield: "You're still here!"

Why did Odie put candles on the toilet?
He wanted to have a birthday potty!

Does Garfield eat too much on his birthday?
Garfield eats too much *every* day!

What party game do rabbits like to play?
Musical Hares.

What do you give a nine-hundred-pound gorilla for his
    birthday?
I don't know, but you'd better hope he likes it!

What song should you sing to a wildebeest on his
    birthday?
"Happy Birthday To Gnu!"

"Doctor, I get heartburn every time I eat birthday
    cake."
"Next time, take off the candles."

Nermal: "Garfield, did you go shopping for my birth-
day present?"
Garfield: "Yeah, and I found the perfect thing."
Nermal: "What thing is that?"
Garfield: "Nothing!"

Did you hear about the flag's birthday?
It was a flappy one!

Jon: "My birthday's coming, Garfield. Do you know
what I need?"
Garfield: "Yeah, but how do you wrap a life?"

Did you hear about the tree's birthday?
It was a sappy one!

Odie is so dumb, he thinks an agent is someone who
keeps track of your age!

Why won't anyone eat Odie's birthday cake?
Because Odie always slobbers out the candles!

What did the ice cream say to the unhappy cake?
"Hey, what's eating you?"

Jon: "Garfield, do you think my skin is starting to
    show its age?"
Garfield: "I can't tell. There are too many wrinkles."

Garfield: "I'm giving Jon a 'surprised' birthday party."
Arlene: "A 'surprised' birthday party? What's that?"
Garfield: "That's where I invite a bunch of Jon's
    friends, and if any of them come, I'll be sur-
    prised!"

What's the best way to find out an elephant's age?
Check his driver's license.

Did you hear about the dancer's birthday?
It was a tappy one!

How can you tell if an elephant's been to your birthday party?
Look for his footprints in the ice cream.

What are Garfield's two favorite times to party?
Daytime and nighttime!

Why did Garfield put a candle on his tummy?
He was celebrating his girthday!

What does a basketball player do before he blows out his candles?
He makes a swish!

Can an elf blow out all his birthday candles at once?
Who knows? He can't even see over the table!

HAUNTED HOWLERS

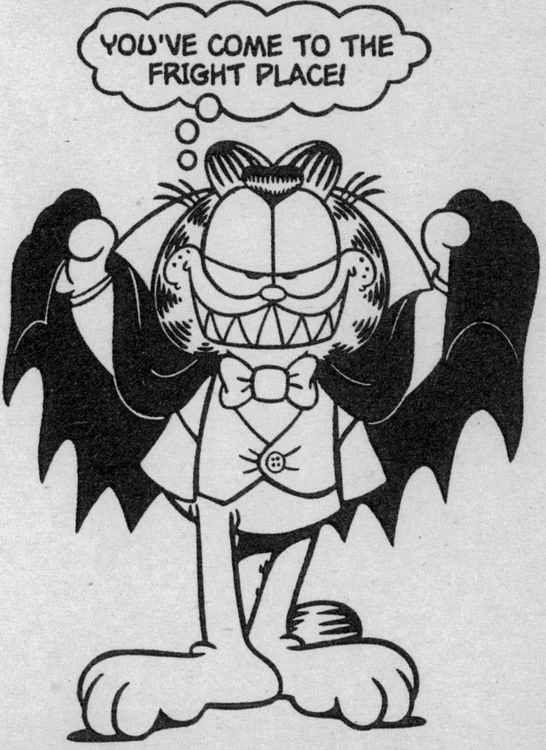
YOU'VE COME TO THE FRIGHT PLACE!

Did you hear about the new ice cream for monsters?
It's called "Cookies and Scream."

What is Garfield's favorite type of Halloween candy?
Lotsa candy.

Why is Odie like a jack-o'-lantern?
They both have empty heads.

What would you get if you crossed Halloween with
    Christmas?
A ghoul Yule!

Knock, knock!
Who's there?
Ivan.
Ivan who?
Ivan to bite your neck!

Where did Garfield take the ghost for lunch?
Pizza Haunt!

Where do werewolves stay when they're on vacation?
At the Howliday Inn!

Where does the Wolfman live?
In a werehouse!

How do zombies celebrate Halloween?
They paint the town dead!

What oinks and drinks blood?
A hampire!

Why are haunted houses so noisy in April?
That's when the ghosts do their spring screaming!

What's orange on the inside and clear on the outside?
A pumpkin in a plastic bag!

What does a vampire take for a cold?
Coffin syrup!

Where do ghost ships like to cruise?
In the Scare-ibbean Sea!

What European capital has the most ghosts?
Boodapest!

Arlene: "Odie certainly looks weird and scary tonight!"
Garfield: "Yeah, and just wait till he puts on his mask!"

What did the ghost serve at his Halloween party?
Hallowieners!

What is a witch's favorite TV show?
Lifestyles of the Witch and Famous!

What do fishermen say on Halloween?
"Trick-or-trout!"

What do birds say on Halloween?
"Trick-or-tweet!"

What's the difference between Garfield's tummy and a
trick-or-treat bag?
You can fill up the bag!

What would you get if you crossed a pumpkin with a
    Magic superstar?
A Shaq-o'-lantern!

Knock, knock!
Who's there?
Trish.
Trish who?
Trish-or-treat!

Student 1: "Did you know that ghosts are protected by
    the Constitution?"
Student 2: "They are?"
Student 1: "Sure. It's in the Bill of Frights!"

Why did the pumpkin wear a football helmet?
Because it was a jock-o'-lantern!

Girl 1: "Can I invite a few friends to your Halloween
    party?"
Girl 2: "Sure. The more, the scarier!"

What do you call a ghost at midnight?
A sheet in the dark!

What did the man say when he saw the long-lost maniac?
"You're a psycho for sore eyes!"

Knock, knock!
Who's there?
Terry.
Terry who?
Terry things happen on Halloween!

Did you hear about the ghost mortician?
He lived in a haunted hearse!

What would you get if you crossed a prehistoric creature with a witch?
A dino-sorceress!

What did the little ghost eat for lunch?
A booloney sandwich!

What do little monsters like to drink?
Ghoul-Aid!

What do you call eyeglasses for a ghost?
Spooktacles!

Where would you find the graves of famous English
    ghouls?
Westmonster Abbey!

How did the bootician style the ghost's hair?
With a scare dryer!

What did the dog say to the skeleton?
"I'd like to get to gnaw you."

Why didn't the little monster go trick-or-treating?
He didn't have a costume.

Girl Monster 1: "I hear you've met the perfect guy."
Girl Monster 2: "Oh yes, he's a bad dream come true!"

Witch 1: "How do you manage to stay in shape?"
Witch 2: "I get a lot of hexercise."

Is it good to drink witch's brew?
Yes, it's very newt-tricious!

Why is a ghost like an empty house?
Because there's no body there!

What happened when the vampire met the werewolf?
They became the best of fiends!

What Central American country has the most spooks?
Ghosta Rica!

What would you get if you crossed the Wolfman with
    a dog?
A werewoof!

What would you get if you crossed Odie with a famous
    phantom?
The Phantom of the Slobbera!

Did you hear about the ghost who went on safari?
He was a big-game haunter!

What game do baby ghosts like to play?
Shriek-a-boo!

What would you get if you crossed Halloween with
    Independence Day?
The Fourth of Ghoul-ly!

Knock, knock!
Who's there?
Fran.
Fran who?
Fran-tom of the Opera!

Why were the trick-or-treaters wearing grass skirts?
Because it was *Hula*ween!

Jon: "This Halloween I'd like to be weird and bizarre."
Garfield: "That's easy. Just be yourself!"

Would seeing a ghost scare the life out of Jon?
No. Jon doesn't have a life.

What's fat, furry, and terrorizes the fridge?
Garfiend!

Where does a vampire keep his Easter candy?
In his Easter casket!

How does a monster begin a fairy tale?
"Once upon a slime ..."

What's worse than a vampire with a toothache?
A skeleton with arthritis!

What happened when the ghost disappeared in the fog?
He was mist.

Where's the most dangerous place to go trick-or-treating?
On the psycho path!

Did you hear about the really stupid horror movie?
It was shudder nonsense!

Did you hear about the Egyptian monster who was a
    terrible driver?
He was a crash mummy!

Did you hear about the starving vampire?
He was all gums!

Why is it tough to compete against a vampire?
Because they're always out for blood!

Vampire 1: "I once went so long without fresh blood
    that I nearly died."
Vampire 2: "How awful!"
Vampire 1: "Yes. Fortunately, I found some in the neck
    of time."

Did you hear about the vampire in Camelot?
He was a bite of the Round Table!

What would you get if you crossed Dracula with Captain Kidd?
A vampirate!

What did the vampire call his girlfriend?
His "vein squeeze"!

What is a werewolf's favorite type of story?
A hairy tale!

Did you hear about the hippie werewolf?
He was fur out, man!

What do you call two witches who live together?
Broommates!

Did you hear about the obnoxious pumpkin?
He was a real jerk-o'-lantern!

What does an Australian witch ride on?
A broomerang!

What would you get if you crossed a witch with a famous movie director?
Steven Spellberg!

BASKET CASE

CASE

This'll crack you up!

Did you hear about the farmer who fed crayons to his chickens?
He wanted them to lay colored eggs!

What did one colored egg say to the other?
"Heard any good yolks lately?"

What is a dog's favorite Easter treat?
Jelly bones!

What has big ears, brings Easter treats, and goes "hippity-BOOM, hippity-BOOM, hippity-BOOM"?
The Easter Elephant.

How does the Easter Bunny stay in shape?
He does lots of hare-obics.

Why didn't Garfield eat his chocolate bunnies right away?
He was waiting for them to multiply!

How should you send a letter to the Easter Bunny?
By hare mail!

Knock, knock!
Who's there?
Philip.
Philip who?
Philip my basket with candy!

What has long ears, brings treats, and leaves a mess on your carpet?
The Easter Odie.

What do you need if your chocolate eggs mysteriously
    disappear?
You need an eggsplanation!

How did the soggy Easter Bunny dry himself?
With a hare dryer!

How is the Easter Bunny like Shaquille O'Neal?
They're both famous for stuffing baskets!

What's red and blue and sogs up your Easter basket?
Colored scrambled eggs!

What's big and purple and hugs your Easter basket?
The Easter Barney!

How does the Easter Bunny paint all of those eggs?
He hires Santa's elves during the off-season.

What happened when the Easter Bunny met the rabbit of his dreams?
They lived hoppily ever after!

Who delivers Easter treats to all the fish in the sea?
The Oyster Bunny!

What will the Easter Bunny be doing after Easter?
One to three for breaking and entering.

How do you catch the Easter Bunny?
Hide in the bushes and make a noise like a carrot!

Jon: "Garfield, why are you stuffing all that Easter candy into your mouth?"
Garfield: "Because it doesn't taste as good if I stuff it in my ears."

Did you hear the one about the fifty-pound jelly bean?
It's pretty hard to swallow!

Garfield: "Nermal, would you like something from my
    Easter basket?
Nermal: "Sure!"
Garfield: "Here. Have some plastic grass."

Jon: "Why is Odie studying his Easter candy?"
Garfield: "He's trying to decide which came first—the
    chocolate chicken or the chocolate egg!"

Did you hear the one about the Easter Bunny who sat
    on a bee?
It's a tender tail!

What happened when the Easter Bunny caught his
    head in the fan?
It took ears off his life!

What would you get if you crossed the Easter Bunny
    with a leprechaun?
The Easter Blarney!

Why did Odie drive the lawn mower over his Easter
    basket?
He thought the plastic grass was growing too high!

Why do we paint Easter eggs?
Because it's easier than trying to wallpaper them!

Why was Odie sitting in his Easter basket?
He was trying to hatch his peanut butter eggs!

What's the difference between Garfield and a jelly
    bean?
You won't get a hernia trying to lift a jelly bean.

What's the difference between Odie and a marshmallow chick?
One has a soft, mushy head, and the other is a piece of candy.

Knock, knock!
Who's there?
Chuck.
Chuck who?
Chuck-olate bunny!

Knock, knock!
Who's there?
Hedda.
Hedda who?
Hedda marshmallow egg for you, but Garfield ate it!

Who is the Easter Bunny's favorite movie actor?
Rabbit De Niro!

Does the Easter Bunny like baseball?
Oh, yes. He's a rabbit fan!

What's pink, has five toes, and is carried by the Easter
   Bunny?
His lucky people's foot!

What's long and stylish and full of cats?
The Easter Purrade!

Knock, knock!
Who's there?
Candy.
Candy who?
Candy Easter Bunny carry all dose treats in one bas-
   ket?

What has long ears, four legs, and is worn on your
   head?
An Easter bunnet!

Boy 1: "How did you get that bruise on your arm?"
Boy 2: "I ate some Easter candy."
Boy 1: "Eating Easter candy won't give you a bruise."
Boy 2: "It will if it's your big brother's candy!"

What would you get if you crossed the Easter Bunny
   with an overstressed person?
An Easter basket case!

What's yellow, has long ears, and grows on trees?
The Easter Bunana!

Why does Peter Cottontail hop down the bunny trail?
Because his parents wouldn't let him borrow the car!

What's soft and white and rolls down the bunny trail?
Peter Cottonball!

Why is Easter like whipped cream and a cherry?
Because it's always on a sundae!

What does a Chinese restaurant serve for Easter?
Colored eggrolls!

A man wanted an Easter pet for his daughter. He looked at a baby chick and a baby duck. They were both very cute, but he decided to buy the baby chick. Do you know why? The baby chick was a little cheeper!

Why did the Easter Bunny have to fire the duck? Because he kept quacking all the eggs!

What is the Easter Bunny's favorite state capital? Albunny, New York!

What would you get if you crossed the Easter Bunny with a famous French general?
Napoleon Bunnyparte!

Where did the Easter Bunny go to college? Johns *Hop*kins!

Did you hear about the lady whose house was infested
    with Easter eggs?
She had to call an eggs-terminator!

What is the Easter Bunny's favorite sport?
Basket-ball, of course!

Why was the Easter Bunny so upset?
He was having a bad hare day!

Jon: "Garfield, what is this mess in the frying pan?"
Garfield: "Guess what, Jon—you can't fry a chocolate
    chicken!"

What would you get if you crossed a skunk with a type
    of Easter candy?
Smelly beans!

What is the Easter Bunny's favorite kind of story?
A cotton tale!

Where does the Easter Bunny go when he needs a
    new tail?
To a re-tail store!

What's the difference between the Easter Bunny and
    Odie?
One's a hare-head and the other's an air-head!

What would you get if you crossed the Easter Bunny
    with Chinese food?
Hop suey!

HAPPY WHATEVER!

THE JEST OF THE REST!

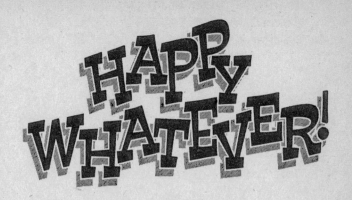

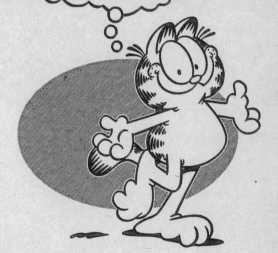

GROUNDHOGGING THE SPOTLIGHT

What's the difference between a woodchuck and Garfield?
One's a groundhog and the other's a round hog!

On Groundhog Day what does it mean if the groundhog sees Odie?
You'll have six more weeks of stupidity!

What does it mean if the groundhog sees Jon?
Six more geeks of winter!

What would you get if you crossed the groundhog with Garfield?
A groundhog who sleeps until June!

What would you get if you crossed February 2 with a puppy?
Ground-dog Day!

What happened when the groundhog met the dog-catcher?
He became a pound hog!

What happens if the ground *log* sees its shadow?
We'll have six more weeks of splinters!

Why was the groundhog depressed about his den?
He was having a bad lair day!

What would you get if you crossed February 2 with a Christmas drink?
Ground Nog Day!

What's green, has four legs, and jumps out of its hole on February 2?
The ground frog!

IT'S ABE, BY GEORGE

What would you get if you crossed a gorilla with the sixteenth U.S. president?
Ape Lincoln!

Why did Abe Lincoln grow a beard?
He wanted to look like that guy on the five-dollar bill.

What would you get if you crossed the sixteenth president with a famous slugger?
Babe Lincoln!

Did Lincoln know that the North would win the Civil War?
After a while, he took it for Grant-ed!

Teacher: "John, do you know Lincoln's Gettysburg Address?"

Student: "No, Miss Frump. I thought he lived in Washington!"

Why did Lincoln wear a tall, black hat?
To keep his head warm!

What U.S. president had long legs, a beard, and an unusual smell?
Abraham Stincoln!

Why was Abraham Lincoln born in a log cabin?
Because it was too cold to be born outside!

Why is Abraham Lincoln like a bloodhound tracking someone?
They're both on the (s)cent!

Why did they call Lincoln "Honest Abe"?
Because that's what it said on all his campaign buttons.

What would you get if you crossed Garfield with the
	first U.S. president?
Large Washington!

Why did George Washington have trouble sleeping?
Because he couldn't lie.

What do you call George Washington's false teeth?
Presidentures!

What would you get if you crossed George Washing-
	ton with Nermal?
The Bother of His Country.

In what way was George Washington like Jon Arbuckle?
In *no* way, thankfully!

What would you get if you crossed the first U.S. president with an animated character?
George Washingtoon!

Was General Washington a handsome man?
Yes, he was George-eous!

What would George Washington be if he were alive today?
Really, really, really old!

Did you hear the one about the crooked George Washington?
He committed Valley Forgery!

How did George Washington speak to his army?
In general terms!

JUST FOOLING AROUND

What do you get if you cross Odie with a prankster's
     holiday?
April Drool's Day!

Knock, knock!
Who's there?
Noah.
Noah who?
Noah body ... April Fool's!

Why is everyone so tired on April 1?
Because they've just finished a long March!

What would you get if you crossed Halloween with
     April 1?
April Ghoul's Day!

Knock, knock!
Who's there?
Noah.
Noah who?
Noah something? It's still April Fool's!

What's the best day for monkey business?
The first of Ape-ril!

Does Garfield know all about April 1?
Yes, he's fooly aware of it!

What's the difference between Thanksgiving and April
    Fool's Day?
On one you're thankful and on the other you're prank-
    ful!

Knock, knock!
Who's there?
Noah.
Noah who?
Noah fooling this time . . . it's really me!

What monster plays the most April Fool's jokes?
Prankenstein!

LET ME PLANT ONE ON YA!

Did you hear the one about Arbor Day?
It'll leaf you laughing!

Did you hear the one about the oak tree?
It's acorny one!

Did you hear the one about the redwood?
It's tree-mendous!

Why was the pine tree sent to its room?
Because it was being knotty!

Why did Odie give the tree some aspirin?
Because he heard it was a *syca*more!

What kind of tree is often found in the kitchen?
A pantry!

Why did Odie plant a board and nails on Arbor Day?
He was trying to grow a tree house!

What is Garfield's favorite type of tree?
A pastry!

Why was the tree drooling?
It was a dogwood.

What does Garfield call a day of planting trees with
     Jon?
Arbore Day!

RED, WHITE, AND WACKY

What's red, white, blue and yellow?
The Star-Spangled Banana!

How is a flag like Santa Claus?
They both hang out at the pole!

What's the difference between June 14 and a day when
   Jon cooks?
One's a flag day and the other's a gag day!

What would you get if you crossed the American flag
   with Garfield?
The Stars and Gripes!

What did the patriotic dog do on Flag Day?
He flagged his tail!

Teacher: "How did the Founding Fathers decide on
our country's flag?"
Student: "I guess they took a flag poll!"

Teacher: "Jenny, what do you know that has stars and
stripes?"
Jenny: "A movie about a zebra!"

What would you get if you crossed a famous march
tune with Jon and his friends?
"Stars and Twerps Forever"!

What would you get if you crossed the Stars and
Stripes with a cookie?
A Flag Newton!

What's the difference between Flag Day and Garfield's
    birthday?
Five days!

GIGGLE WHILE YOU WORK

Dad: "Most people don't have to work today, because
    it's Labor Day."
Son: "If they're not working, shouldn't it be 'No-Labor'
    Day?"

What does Garfield usually do on Labor Day?
As little as possible, just like every day!

How is Labor Day like a visit from Nermal?
They both mark the end of a good time!

Why did Odie think someone was about to have a
    baby?
Because Jon said it was Labor Day!

Did you hear the one about Labor Day?
It works for me!

HEY! DISCOVER THIS!

Where did Columbus first land in America?
On his feet!

Who was the first cat to discover America?
Christopher Col?umpuss!

How was Columbus's ship like an avid shopper?
They're both driven by sales!

What's the difference between one of Columbus's sailors and Odie?
One left his Spain behind and the other left his brain behind!

What would you get if you crossed October 12 with Halloween?

Ghoulumbus Day!

STRIPS, SPECIALS, OR BESTSELLING BOOKS...
GARFIELD'S ON EVERYONE'S MENU!
Don't miss even one episode in the tubby tabby's hilarious series!

Call toll free 1-800-733-3000 to order by phone and use your major credit card. Or use this coupon to order by mail.

__GARFIELD AT LARGE	345-32013-1	$6.95
__GARFIELD GAINS WEIGHT	345-32008-5	$6.95
__GARFIELD BIGGER THAN LIFE	345-32007-7	$6.95
__GARFIELD WEIGHS IN	345-32010-7	$6.95
__GARFIELD TAKES THE CAKE	345-32009-3	$8.95
__GARFIELD EATS HIS HEART OUT	345-32018-2	$6.95
__GARFIELD SITS AROUND THE HOUSE	345-32011-5	$6.95
__GARFIELD TIPS THE SCALES	345-33580-5	$6.95
__GARFIELD LOSES HIS FEET	345-31805-6	$6.95
__GARFIELD MAKES IT BIG	345-31928-1	$6.95
__GARFIELD ROLLS ON	345-32634-2	$6.95
__GARFIELD OUT TO LUNCH	345-33118-4	$6.95
__GARFIELD FOOD FOR THOUGHT	345-34129-5	$6.95
__GARFIELD SWALLOWS HIS PRIDE	345-34725-0	$6.95
__GARFIELD WORLDWIDE	345-35158-4	$6.95
__GARFIELD ROUNDS OUT	345-35388-9	$6.95
__GARFIELD CHEWS THE FAT	345-35956-9	$6.95
__GARFIELD GOES TO WAIST	345-36430-9	$6.95
__GARFIELD HANGS OUT	345-36835-5	$6.95
__GARFIELD TAKES UP SPACE	345-37029-5	$6.95
__GARFIELD SAYS A MOUTHFUL	345-37368-5	$6.95
__GARFIELD BY THE POUND	345-37579-3	$6.95
__GARFIELD KEEPS HIS CHINS UP	345-37959-4	$6.95
__GARFIELD FAT CAT THREE PACK	345-38385-0	$9.95
__GARFIELD TAKES HIS LICKS	345-38170-X	$6.95
__GARFIELD HITS THE BIG TIME	345-38332-X	$6.95

GARFIELD AT HIS SUNDAY BEST!

__GARFIELD TREASURY	345-32106-5	$11.95
__THE SECOND GARFIELD TREASURY	345-33276-6	$10.95
__THE THIRD GARFIELD TREASURY	345-32635-0	$11.00
__THE FOURTH GARFIELD TREASURY	345-34726-9	$10.95
__THE FIFTH GARFIELD TREASURY	345-36268-3	$12.00
__THE SIXTH GARFIELD TREASURY	345-37367-7	$10.95

Name_____
Address _____
City_____State_____Zip _____

Please send me the BALLANTINE BOOKS I have checked above.

I am enclosing	$____
plus	
Postage & handling*	$____
Sales tax (where applicable)	$____
Total amount enclosed	$____

*Add $2 for the first book and 50¢ for each additional book.

Send check or money order (no cash or CODs) to:
Ballantine Mail Sales, 400 Hahn Road, Westminster, MD 21157.

Prices and numbers subject to change without notice.
Valid in the U.S. only.
All orders subject to availability.   DAVIS2